Text by Ines de la Fressange and Sophie Gachet
Illustrations by Ines de la Fressange

Flammarion

Design
Noémie Levain

Translation
Louise Lalaurie Rogers

Copyediting
Lindsay Porter

Typesetting
Gravemaker+Scott

Printed in China by Toppan Leefung

© Flammarion, SA, Paris, 2013
ISBN: 978-2-08-020151-5
Dépôt légal: 06/2013

Name

HOME

Address

Telephone   Cell phone

e-mail

WORK

Address

Telephone

e-mail

IMPORTANT INFORMATION

Driver's license ID

Passport number

Primary care physician

Telephone

Blood type

In case of emergency, please contact

CALENDAR 2014

JANUARY

S	M	T	W	T	F	S
			1	2	3	4
5	6	7	8	9	10	11
12	13	14	15	16	17	18
19	20	21	22	23	24	25
26	27	28	29	30	31	

FEBRUARY

S	M	T	W	T	F	S
						1
2	3	4	5	6	7	8
9	10	11	12	13	14	15
16	17	18	19	20	21	22
23	24	25	26	27	28	

MARCH

S	M	T	W	T	F	S
						1
2	3	4	5	6	7	8
9	10	11	12	13	14	15
16	17	18	19	20	21	22
23	24	25	26	27	28	29
30	31					

APRIL

S	M	T	W	T	F	S
		1	2	3	4	5
6	7	8	9	10	11	12
13	14	15	16	17	18	19
20	21	22	23	24	25	26
27	28	29	30			

MAY

S	M	T	W	T	F	S
				1	2	3
4	5	6	7	8	9	10
11	12	13	14	15	16	17
18	19	20	21	22	23	24
25	26	27	28	29	30	31

JUNE

S	M	T	W	T	F	S
1	2	3	4	5	6	7
8	9	10	11	12	13	14
15	16	17	18	19	20	21
22	23	24	25	26	27	28
29	30					

JULY

S	M	T	W	T	F	S
		1	2	3	4	5
6	7	8	9	10	11	12
13	14	15	16	17	18	19
20	21	22	23	24	25	26
27	28	29	30	31		

AUGUST

S	M	T	W	T	F	S
					1	2
3	4	5	6	7	8	9
10	11	12	13	14	15	16
17	18	19	20	21	22	23
24	25	26	27	28	29	30
31						

SEPTEMBER

S	M	T	W	T	F	S
	1	2	3	4	5	6
7	8	9	10	11	12	13
14	15	16	17	18	19	20
21	22	23	24	25	26	27
28	29	30				

OCTOBER

S	M	T	W	T	F	S
			1	2	3	4
5	6	7	8	9	10	11
12	13	14	15	16	17	18
19	20	21	22	23	24	25
26	27	28	29	30	31	

NOVEMBER

S	M	T	W	T	F	S
						1
2	3	4	5	6	7	8
9	10	11	12	13	14	15
16	17	18	19	20	21	22
23	24	25	26	27	28	29
30						

DECEMBER

S	M	T	W	T	F	S
	1	2	3	4	5	6
7	8	9	10	11	12	13
14	15	16	17	18	19	20
21	22	23	24	25	26	27
28	29	30	31			

CALENDAR 2015

JANUARY

S	M	T	W	T	F	S
				1	2	3
4	5	6	7	8	9	10
11	12	13	14	15	16	17
18	19	20	21	22	23	24
25	26	27	28	29	30	31

FEBRUARY

S	M	T	W	T	F	S
1	2	3	4	5	6	7
8	9	10	11	12	13	14
15	16	17	18	19	20	21
22	23	24	25	26	27	28

MARCH

S	M	T	W	T	F	S
1	2	3	4	5	6	7
8	9	10	11	12	13	14
15	16	17	18	19	20	21
22	23	24	25	26	27	28
29	30	31				

APRIL

S	M	T	W	T	F	S
			1	2	3	4
5	6	7	8	9	10	11
12	13	14	15	16	17	18
19	20	21	22	23	24	25
26	27	28	29	30		

MAY

S	M	T	W	T	F	S
					1	2
3	4	5	6	7	8	9
10	11	12	13	14	15	16
17	18	19	20	21	22	23
24	25	26	27	28	29	30
31						

JUNE

S	M	T	W	T	F	S
	1	2	3	4	5	6
7	8	9	10	11	12	13
14	15	16	17	18	19	20
21	22	23	24	25	26	27
28	29	30				

JULY

S	M	T	W	T	F	S
			1	2	3	4
5	6	7	8	9	10	11
12	13	14	15	16	17	18
19	20	21	22	23	24	25
26	27	28	29	30	31	

AUGUST

S	M	T	W	T	F	S
						1
2	3	4	5	6	7	8
9	10	11	12	13	14	15
16	17	18	19	20	21	22
23	24	25	26	27	28	29
30	31					

SEPTEMBER

S	M	T	W	T	F	S
		1	2	3	4	5
6	7	8	9	10	11	12
13	14	15	16	17	18	19
20	21	22	23	24	25	26
27	28	29	30			

OCTOBER

S	M	T	W	T	F	S
				1	2	3
4	5	6	7	8	9	10
11	12	13	14	15	16	17
18	19	20	21	22	23	24
25	26	27	28	29	30	31

NOVEMBER

S	M	T	W	T	F	S
1	2	3	4	5	6	7
8	9	10	11	12	13	14
15	16	17	18	19	20	21
22	23	24	25	26	27	28
29	30					

DECEMBER

S	M	T	W	T	F	S
		1	2	3	4	5
6	7	8	9	10	11	12
13	14	15	16	17	18	19
20	21	22	23	24	25	26
27	28	29	30	31		

notes

NEW YEAR'S RESOLUTION:

No resolutions!
Why start 2014
feeling guilty
and inadequate?

Sunday ✴ 29

Monday ✴ 30

EW YEAR'S EVE

Tuesday ✴ 31

EW YEAR'S DAY

Wednesday ✴ 1

nd JANUARY (Scotland)

Thursday ✴ 2

Friday ✴ 3

Saturday ✴ 4

notes

Wear it up, wear it down,
but wear your hair LONG.
THE look for 2014.

Sunday ✳ 5

EPIPHANY

Monday ✳ 6

Tuesday ✳ 7

Wednesday ✳ 8

Thursday ✳ 9

Friday ✳ 10

Saturday ✳ 11

notes

**TEAM YOUR CHUNKY
CARDIGAN WITH A LACE BRA.**
Central heating for the man in your life.

Sunday ✳ 12

Monday ✳ 13

Tuesday ✳ 14

FULL MOON

Wednesday ✳ 15

Thursday ✳ 16

Friday ✳ 17

Saturday ✳ 18

notes

For the perfect pair of riding
boots try . . . genuine riding boots.
From a sports supplier
near you.

Sunday * 19

MARTIN LUTHER KING, JR. DAY (US)   Monday * 20

Tuesday * 21

Wednesday * 22

Thursday * 23

Friday * 24

Saturday * 25

notes

A first date when it's 14°F (-10°C) outside?
Grin and bear it—wear your warmest blazer,
and stock up on vitamin C!

TRALIA DAY

Sunday ✳ 26

TRALIA DAY OBSERVED

Monday ✳ 27

Tuesday ✳ 28

Wednesday ✳ 29

Thursday ✳ 30

ESE NEW YEAR

Friday ✳ 31

Saturday ✳ 1

notes

Liven up those long winter evenings
with a good, old-fashioned fight.
Smashed plates are a great excuse
to go shopping.

UNDHOG DAY (US)

Sunday ✳ 2

Monday ✳ 3

Tuesday ✳ 4

Wednesday ✳ 5

NGI DAY (New Zealand)

Thursday ✳ 6

Friday ✳ 7

Saturday ✳ 8

notes

It's Valentine's Day!
Remind the man in your life
that diamonds are still
an investor's best friend.

Sunday ✶ 9

Monday ✶ 10

Tuesday ✶ 11

Wednesday ✶ 12

Thursday ✶ 13

T. VALENTINE'S DAY • FULL MOON

Friday ✶ 14

Saturday ✶ 15

notes

✳ *Enjoy a drop of Bordeaux.*
THE color for your coat, clutch, or best dress
is very welcome in a wine glass, too.

Sunday ✳ 16

PRESIDENTS' DAY (US)   Monday ✳ 17

Tuesday ✳ 18

Wednesday ✳ 19

Thursday ✳ 20

Friday ✳ 21

Saturday ✳ 22

notes

Change your home lighting scheme:
Spray-paint your lampshades!

Sunday ✳ 23

Monday ✳ 24

Tuesday ✳ 25

Wednesday ✳ 26

Thursday ✳ 27

Friday ✳ 28

Saturday ✳ 1

notes

DRESSING TO CATCH HIS ATTENTION?

Nothing beats black leather trousers. Or (for other types of men) a pencil skirt.

✳

READ ACROSS AMERICA DAY

Sunday ✳ 2

LABOUR DAY (Western Australia)

Monday ✳ 3

MARDI GRAS (SHROVE TUESDAY)

Tuesday ✳ 4

ASH WEDNESDAY

Wednesday ✳ 5

Thursday ✳ 6

Friday ✳ 7

Saturday ✳ 8

notes

Every day, write down the best thing that's happened to you in a notebook. Read it back: you'll soon see it's a wonderful life.

DAYLIGHT SAVING TIME BEGINS (US & Canada)

Sunday ✳ 9

LABOUR DAY (Victoria, Australia)

Monday ✳ 10

Tuesday ✳ 11

Wednesday ✳ 12

Thursday ✳ 13

Friday ✳ 14

Saturday ✳ 15

notes

Convinced you have nothing to wear?
You've just fallen out of love with your
wardrobe. So, donate it, sell it, dye it. . . .

FULL MOON

Sunday ✳ 16

ST. PATRICK'S DAY

Monday ✳ 17

Tuesday ✳ 18

Wednesday ✳ 19

FIRST DAY OF SPRING

Thursday ✳ 20

Friday ✳ 21

Saturday ✳ 22

notes

Transform your spaghetti
and (store-bought) pesto:
add green vegetables—
chopped zucchini or peas,
cooked with the pasta—
for instant culinary chic.

Sunday * 23

Monday * 24

Tuesday * 25

Wednesday * 26

Thursday * 27

Friday * 28

Saturday * 29

notes

Everyone has a girlfriend they keep
promising to meet for lunch.
So . . . give her a call
and make a date!

DAYLIGHT SAVING TIME BEGINS (UK & Ireland)
MOTHER'S DAY (UK & Ireland)

Sunday ✳ 30

Monday ✳ 31

APRIL FOOL'S DAY

Tuesday ✳ 1

Wednesday ✳ 2

Thursday ✳ 3

Friday ✳ 4

Saturday ✳ 5

notes

As playwright Eugène Ionesco said:
"Trying to be up-to-date means
you're already passé."
The reason why the latest trend
for leather shorts should be resisted
at all costs.

AYLIGHT SAVING TIME ENDS (Australia, as applicable)

Sunday ✳ 6

Monday ✳ 7

Tuesday ✳ 8

Wednesday ✳ 9

Thursday ✳ 10

Friday ✳ 11

Saturday ✳ 12

notes

REACHING FOR A GOAL?

→ Write it down and be sure to do one thing to get you there every day.

PALM SUNDAY

Sunday ✳ 13

PASSOVER (Begins at Sundown)

Monday ✳ 14

FULL MOON

Tuesday ✳ 15

Wednesday ✳ 16

Thursday ✳ 17

GOOD FRIDAY

Friday ✳ 18

Saturday ✳ 19

notes

**SMALL WAYS TO SAVE
THE PLANET:**

Buy a secondhand watch
and tell everyone
"It's a collector's piece."

EASTER SUNDAY • ORTHODOX EASTER

Sunday ✳ 20

EASTER MONDAY (UK [except Scotland], Ireland,
Australia, New Zealand & Canada)

Monday ✳ 21

EARTH DAY

Tuesday ✳ 22

Wednesday ✳ 23

Thursday ✳ 24

ANZAC DAY (Australia and New Zealand Army Corps)

Friday ✳ 25

Saturday ✳ 26

notes

*Ne'er cast a clout till May is out!
Even if he can't wait to see you
out of your winter wrappings.*

FREEDOM DAY (South Africa)

Sunday ✳ 27

Monday ✳ 28

Tuesday ✳ 29

Wednesday ✳ 30

MAY DAY

Thursday ✳ 1

Friday ✳ 2

Saturday ✳ 3

MAY

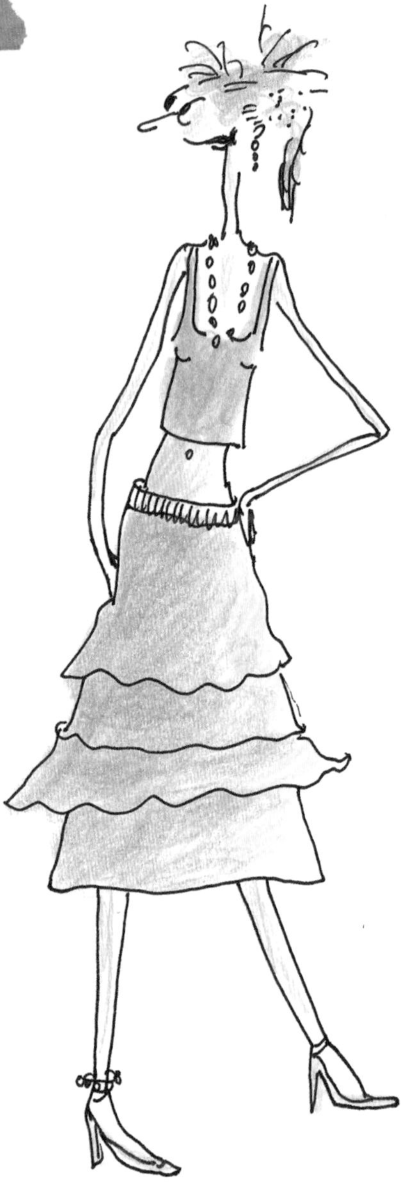

Swimwear ahead. Need to lose 6 lbs?
Dance around the kitchen while baking cookies.

Sunday ✳ 4

ARLY MAY BANK HOLIDAY (UK & Ireland)
CINCO DE MAYO

Monday ✳ 5

Tuesday ✳ 6

Wednesday ✳ 7

Thursday ✳ 8

Friday ✳ 9

Saturday ✳ 10

notes

MOTHER'S DAY (Except UK & Ireland)

Sunday * 11

Monday * 12

Tuesday * 13

FULL MOON

Wednesday * 14

Thursday * 15

Friday * 16

Saturday * 17

notes

WORTH KNOWING:
Making love lowers
your stress levels
and raises life expectancy.

Sunday * 18

VICTORIA DAY (Canada)

Monday * 19

Tuesday * 20

Wednesday * 21

Thursday * 22

Friday * 23

Saturday * 24

notes

Invest in some self-tanning cream —
instant sunshine guaranteed.

Sunday ✳ 25

MEMORIAL DAY (US) • SPRING BANK HOLIDAY (UK)   Monday ✳ 26

Tuesday ✳ 27

Wednesday ✳ 28

Thursday ✳ 29

Friday ✳ 30

Saturday ✳ 31

notes

＊ Stormy weather? Organize a picnic
on the floor at home. Don't forget
the red checkered picnic blanket.

Sunday ✳ 1

QUEEN'S BIRTHDAY (New Zealand)
JUNE BANK HOLIDAY (Ireland)

Monday ✳ 2

Tuesday ✳ 3

Wednesday ✳ 4

Thursday ✳ 5

Friday ✳ 6

Saturday ✳ 7

notes

TIRED OF THAT SAME OLD LITTLE BLACK DRESS?
Try it with floral print accessories, and fall in love
with your little black dress all over again.

PENTECOST

Sunday ✳ 8

QUEEN'S BIRTHDAY (Australia, except Western Australia)

Monday ✳ 9

Tuesday ✳ 10

Wednesday ✳ 11

Thursday ✳ 12

FULL MOON

Friday ✳ 13

Saturday ✳ 14

notes

*Invite your friends
chez vous
and hand round
the best local take-out
menus. Order in,
sit back, and enjoy
your dinner party.*

ATHER'S DAY (Except Australia & New Zealand)
RINITY SUNDAY

Sunday ✳ 15

Monday ✳ 16

Tuesday ✳ 17

Wednesday ✳ 18

Thursday ✳ 19

Friday ✳ 20

RST DAY OF SUMMER

Saturday ✳ 21

notes

THE BEST WAY TO TRAVEL LIGHT?
Two small wheeled suitcases
are better than one big one.

Sunday ✶ 22

Monday ✶ 23

Tuesday ✶ 24

Wednesday ✶ 25

Thursday ✶ 26

Friday ✶ 27

Saturday ✶ 28

notes

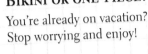

BIKINI OR ONE-PIECE?

You're already on vacation?
Stop worrying and enjoy!

Sunday ✳ 29

Monday ✳ 30

ANADA DAY

Tuesday ✳ 1

Wednesday ✳ 2

Thursday ✳ 3

IDEPENDENCE DAY (US)

Friday ✳ 4

Saturday ✳ 5

notes

THE BEST LOOK, BEACHSIDE?

→ Sunglasses. Always. You'll save money
on eye-cream this winter.

Sunday ✳ 6

Monday ✳ 7

Tuesday ✳ 8

Wednesday ✳ 9

Thursday ✳ 10

Friday ✳ 11

RANGEMEN'S DAY (Northern Ireland) • **FULL MOON**   Saturday ✳ 12

notes

If you have to take just one pair of shoes on vacation,
make it . . . a little pair of flat, gold, strappy sandals.
Perfect for night and day.

Sunday ✳ 13

ORANGEMEN'S DAY OBSERVED (Northern Ireland)
BASTILLE DAY

Monday ✳ 14

Tuesday ✳ 15

Wednesday ✳ 16

Thursday ✳ 17

Friday ✳ 18

Saturday ✳ 19

notes

Brush—but don't wash—your
hair when you're back from
the beach. Salt adds volume.

Sunday ✳ 20

Monday ✳ 21

Tuesday ✳ 22

Wednesday ✳ 23

Thursday ✳ 24

Friday ✳ 25

Saturday ✳ 26

notes

✱ Send a postcard to an unlikely person. They'll be delighted, not surprised.

Sunday ✳ 27

Monday ✳ 28

Tuesday ✳ 29

Wednesday ✳ 30

Thursday ✳ 31

Friday ✳ 1

Saturday ✳ 2

notes

Invest in a pair of espadrilles from the market.
And you can wear them around the house in January,
for that "on vacation" feeling.

Sunday ✳ 3

SUMMER BANK HOLIDAY (Scotland & Ireland)   Monday ✳ 4

Tuesday ✳ 5

Wednesday ✳ 6

Thursday ✳ 7

Friday ✳ 8

Saturday ✳ 9

notes

Just like 2013, August 11—Ines's birthday—is hereby declared a national holiday! (OK, last year it fell on a Sunday.... take the day off this year!)

FULL MOON

Sunday ✳ 10

Monday ✳ 11

Tuesday ✳ 12

Wednesday ✳ 13

Thursday ✳ 14

ASSUMPTION

Friday ✳ 15

Saturday ✳ 16

notes

Celebrate (don't commiserate)
getting back to your routine: make
cut-outs of your perfect fall wardrobe
from your favorite catalogs and
magazines (even stuff you can't afford).

Sunday * 17

Monday * 18

Tuesday * 19

Wednesday * 20

Thursday * 21

Friday * 22

Saturday * 23

notes

Don't change a thing. Carry your files in your beach basket—you'll have the impression that you can still feel the sand between your toes.

Sunday * 24

SUMMER BANK HOLIDAY (UK, except Scotland)

Monday * 25

Tuesday * 26

Wednesday * 27

Thursday * 28

Friday * 29

Saturday * 30

notes

Wondering whether to buy that wardrobe item?
Ask yourself whether your personal style icon
would wear it? No? Forget it, then!

Sunday ✱ 31

LABOR DAY (US & Canada)

Monday ✱ 1

Tuesday ✱ 2

Wednesday ✱ 3

Thursday ✱ 4

Friday ✱ 5

Saturday ✱ 6

SEPTEMBER

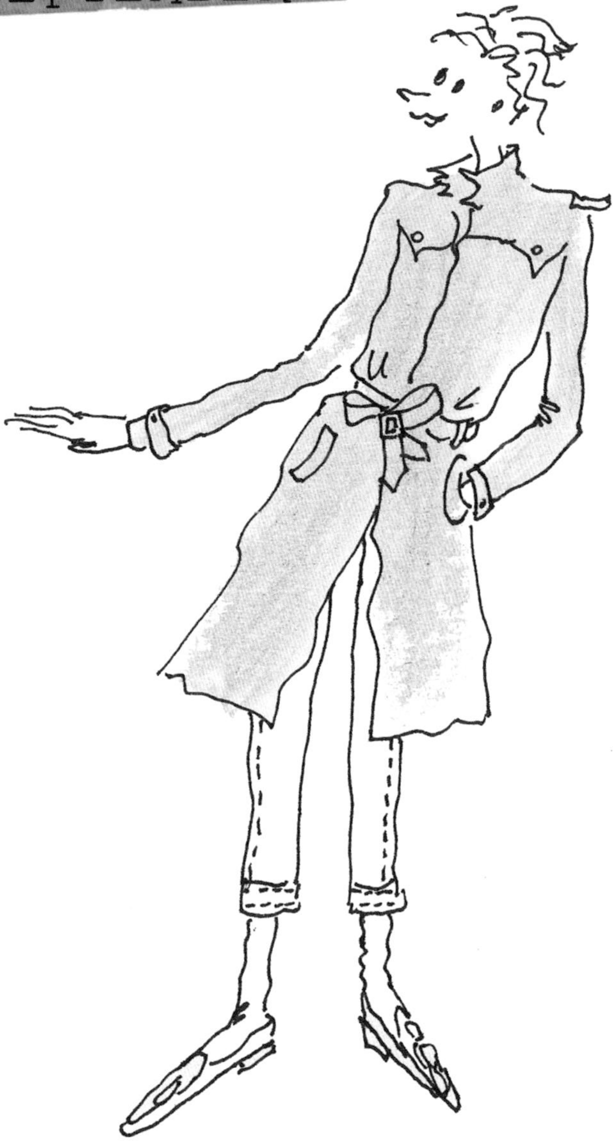

notes

Too soon to light your first log fire?
Fill your living room with multicolored candles
for a warm, festive atmosphere.

ATHER'S DAY (Australia & New Zealand)

Sunday ✳ 7

ULL MOON

Monday ✳ 8

Tuesday ✳ 9

Wednesday ✳ 10

Thursday ✳ 11

Friday ✳ 12

Saturday ✳ 13

notes

Gentlemen prefer women
who don't wear lip gloss.
Just something you need to know,
that's all.

Sunday * 14

Monday * 15

Tuesday * 16

Wednesday * 17

Thursday * 18

Friday * 19

Saturday * 20

notes

Always keep something sparkly
to hand (a T-shirt, a belt, a jacket),
for that last-minute evening invite.
It will transform your business suit.

✳

INTERNATIONAL DAY OF PEACE

Sunday ✳ 21

Monday ✳ 22

FIRST DAY OF AUTUMN

Tuesday ✳ 23

ROSH HASHANAH (Begins at Sundown)

Wednesday ✳ 24

Thursday ✳ 25

Friday ✳ 26

Saturday ✳ 27

notes

Give your watch a makeover: change the strap!

SEPTEMBER–OCTOBER 2014

Sunday ✳ 28

QUEEN'S BIRTHDAY (Western Australia)

Monday ✳ 29

Tuesday ✳ 30

Wednesday ✳ 1

Thursday ✳ 2

YOM KIPPUR (Begins at Sundown)

Friday ✳ 3

Saturday ✳ 4

notes

A GLASS OF CARROT JUICE IN THE
MORNING IS WORTH ANY AMOUNT
OF BROCCOLI AT DINNER.

DAYLIGHT SAVING TIME BEGINS (Australia, as applicable)

Sunday ✳ 5

LABOUR DAY (South Australia, Australian Capital Territory, New South Wales, Queensland)

Monday ✳ 6

Tuesday ✳ 7

FULL MOON

Wednesday ✳ 8

Thursday ✳ 9

Friday ✳ 10

Saturday ✳ 11

notes

Create online albums of all your vacation
photos. If you leave it too long,
you won't remember the names of
the places or the people in them.

Sunday ✳ 12

COLUMBUS DAY (US) • **THANKSGIVING DAY** (Canada)   *Monday* ✳ 13

Tuesday ✳ 14

Wednesday ✳ 15

Thursday ✳ 16

Friday ✳ 17

Saturday ✳ 18

notes

Start saving for your next summer vacation.
Stick a picture of your destination
on the fridge to keep you focused.

Sunday ✳ 19

Monday ✳ 20

Tuesday ✳ 21

Wednesday ✳ 22

Thursday ✳ 23

Friday ✳ 24

Saturday ✳ 25

notes

Cover your sofa
with a throw:
it'll look like new!

DAYLIGHT SAVING TIME ENDS (UK & Ireland)

Sunday ✳ 26

LABOUR DAY (New Zealand)
OCTOBER BANK HOLIDAY (Ireland)

Monday ✳ 27

Tuesday ✳ 28

Wednesday ✳ 29

Thursday ✳ 30

HALLOWEEN

Friday ✳ 31

ALL SAINTS' DAY

Saturday ✳ 1

NOVEMBER

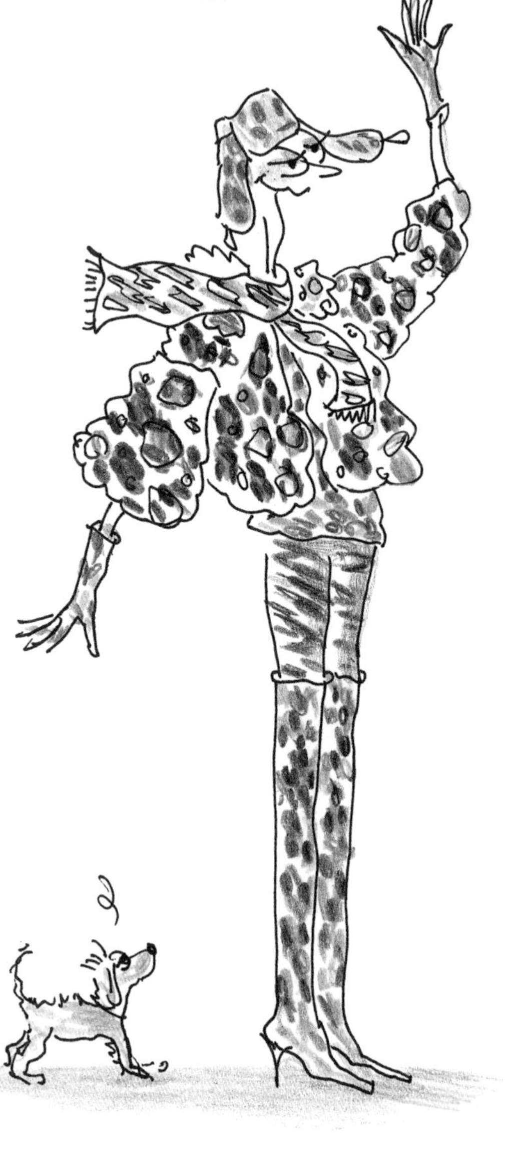

notes

Organize your own home film festival,
with your favorite vintage DVDs
(Wilder, Cukor, Hitchcock, Mankiewicz).
Nostalgia rules!

DAYLIGHT SAVING TIME ENDS (US & Canada)

Sunday ✳ 2

Monday ✳ 3

ELECTION DAY (US)

Tuesday ✳ 4

GUY FAWKES DAY (UK)

Wednesday ✳ 5

FULL MOON

Thursday ✳ 6

Friday ✳ 7

Saturday ✳ 8

The winter sales are a state of mind. Want them now? Hit the stores: so much more choice, so much less crowded!

REMEMBRANCE SUNDAY (UK)

Sunday ✳ 9

Monday ✳ 10

VETERANS' DAY (US) • **REMEMBRANCE DAY** (UK, Canada & Australia)

Tuesday ✳ 11

Wednesday ✳ 12

Thursday ✳ 13

Friday ✳ 14

Saturday ✳ 15

notes

Treat yourself to an
exfoliating treatment
in a real Turkish bath.
A healthy excuse to devour
authentic sweet delights
afterward.

Sunday ✷ 16

Monday ✷ 17

Tuesday ✷ 18

Wednesday ✷ 19

Thursday ✷ 20

Friday ✷ 21

Saturday ✷ 22

notes

The countdown to Christmas begins! Shop now for gifts—you'll avoid the crowds and feel smug when everyone else is panicking two days before Christmas!

Sunday * 23

Monday * 24

Tuesday * 25

Wednesday * 26

THANKSGIVING DAY (US)

Thursday * 27

Friday * 28

Saturday * 29

notes

Gifts for family and friends
are all finished (soap, candles, ties).
Time to treat yourself
(shoes, handbag, bracelet).

✱

ST. ANDREW'S DAY

Sunday ✳ 30

ST. ANDREW'S DAY OBSERVED (Scotland)

Monday ✳ 1

Tuesday ✳ 2

Wednesday ✳ 3

Thursday ✳ 4

Friday ✳ 5

FULL MOON

Saturday ✳ 6

notes

The annual Christmas dilemma:
what to wear while receiving presents?
Avoid jewelry: it may clash with what's
under the wrapping paper.

Sunday ✳ 7

Monday ✳ 8

Tuesday ✳ 9

HUMAN RIGHTS DAY

Wednesday ✳ 10

Thursday ✳ 11

Friday ✳ 12

Saturday ✳ 13

notes

WINTER'S HERE: SO MAKE LIKE
A POLAR BEAR AND CELEBRATE WITH
A WARM, ALL-WHITE WARDROBE!

Sunday ✷ 14

Monday ✷ 15

HANUKKAH (Begins at Sundown)
DAY OF RECONCILIATION (South Africa)

Tuesday ✷ 16

Wednesday ✷ 17

Thursday ✷ 18

Friday ✷ 19

Saturday ✷ 20

notes

Deck your hall (and your living room, and anywhere else that takes your fancy) with garlands of lights. Why should the tree get all the fun?

FIRST DAY OF WINTER

Sunday ✳ 21

Monday ✳ 22

Tuesday ✳ 23

CHRISTMAS EVE

Wednesday ✳ 24

CHRISTMAS DAY

Thursday ✳ 25

KWANZAA BEGINS • **BOXING DAY** (Canada & UK)
ST. STEPHEN'S DAY (Ireland)

Friday ✳ 26

Saturday ✳ 27

notes

GREET THE NEW YEAR IN STYLE.
Wear every piece
of gold jewelry you
have—for good luck!
Happy 2015!

DECEMBER 2014–JANUARY 2015

Sunday ✱ 28

Monday ✱ 29

Tuesday ✱ 30

NEW YEAR'S EVE

Wednesday ✱ 31

NEW YEAR'S DAY

Thursday ✱ 1

2nd JANUARY (Scotland)

Friday ✱ 2

Saturday ✱ 3

notes

Addresses

A

B

C

D

Addresses

E

F

G

H

Addresses

I

J

K

L

Addresses

M

N

O

P

Addresses

Q

R

S

T

U

V

Addresses

W

X

Y

Z